MW01518011

Follow~the~Dots

Winky Adam

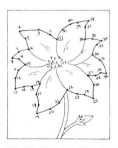

DOVER PUBLICATIONS, INC.

Mineola, New York

Follow the dots and find the flower! And when you've finished the the dot-to-dots pictures, be sure to color them in, for an extra bouquet of flower fun.

Daisy
You'll find this cheerful flower growing in
meadows, pastures, and along roadsides.

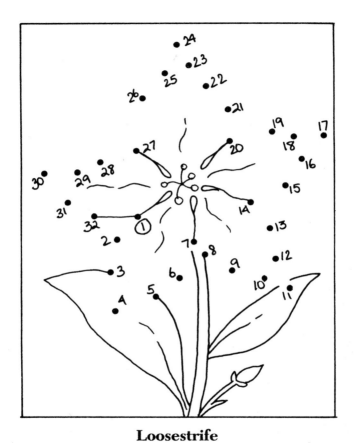

Loosestrife
This little yellow flower is shaped like a star.

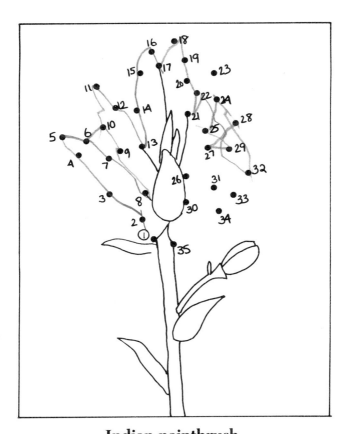

Indian paintbrush
This red, brush-like flower looks like it's
been dipped in paint.

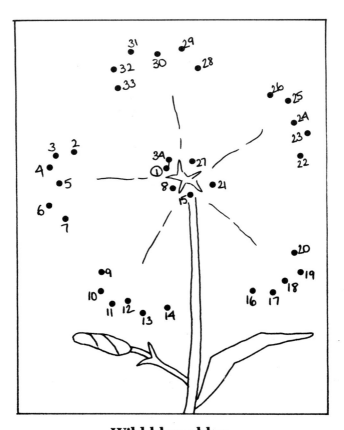

Wild blue phlox
Light blue flowers bloom on top
of this tall plant.

Wood sorrel
This dainty flower grows in the
mountains and woods.

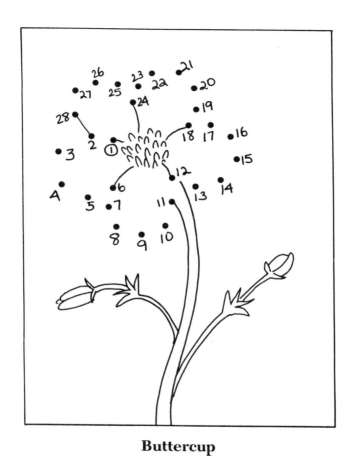

Buttercup
Here's a tiny flower that's the color of butter.

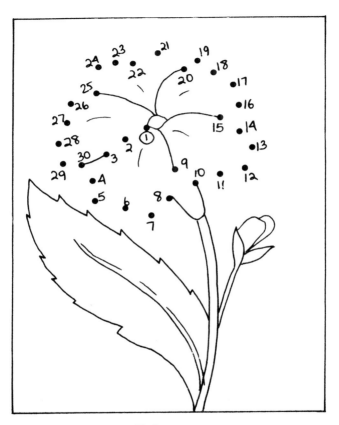

Primrose
This small, cheery flower blooms
in early spring.

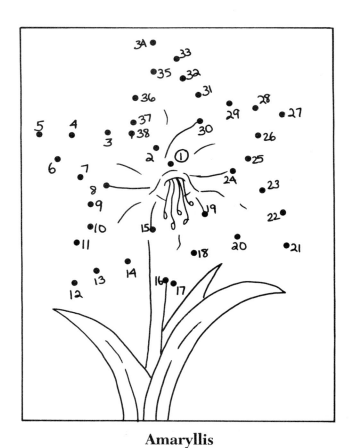

Amaryllis
When kept in a greenhouse, this plant will
bloom with red flowers in the winter.

Marsh marigold
This yellow flower grows in
marshes and meadows.

13

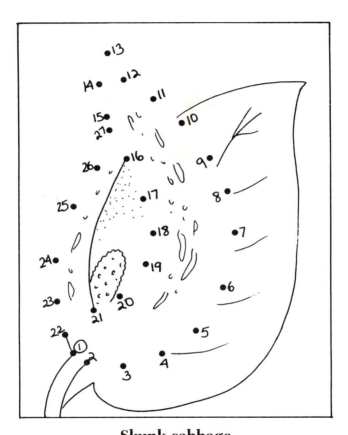

Skunk cabbage
Black bears sometimes eat this flower
in the warm weather.

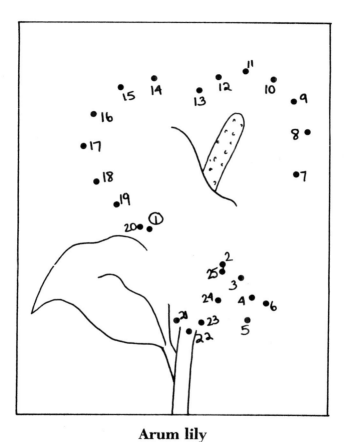

Arum lily
Here's a beautiful white flower that
grows where it's wet.

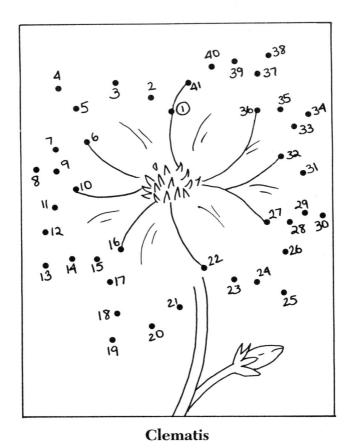

Clematis
This high-climbing vine has
deep purple flowers.

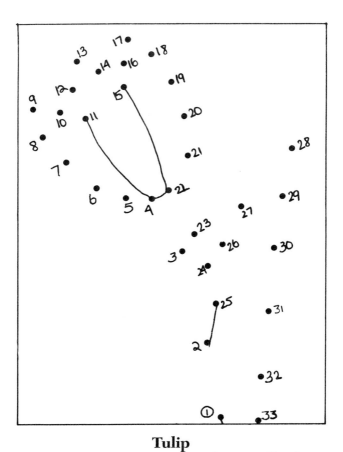

Tulip
This flower, which comes from Holland,
blooms in the spring.

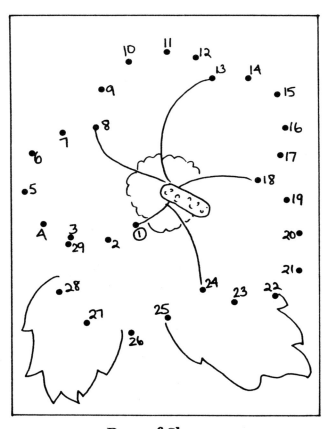

Rose of Sharon
Large rose, purple, or white flowers
bloom on this plant.

18

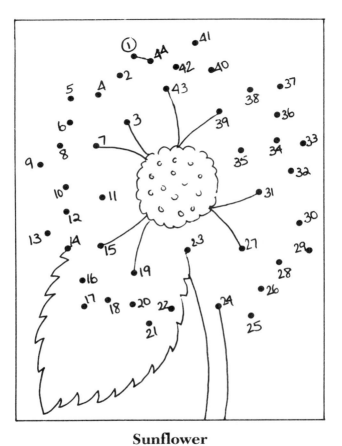

Sunflower
These bright, yellow flowers love the sun.

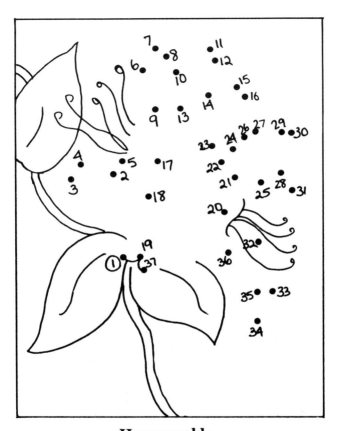

Honeysuckle
This climbing wildflower fills the air
with sweet perfume.

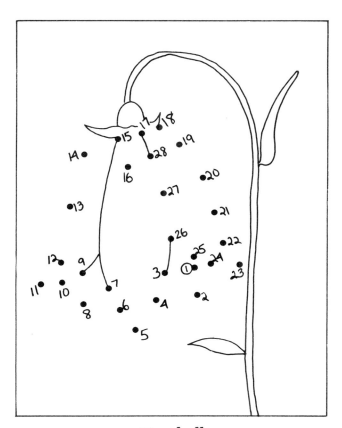

Harebell
These blue flowers look like bells.

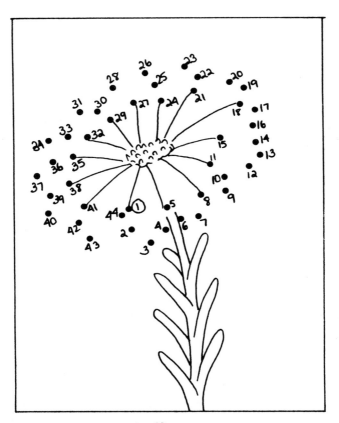

Stiff aster
This bristly flower grows in dry, rocky soil.

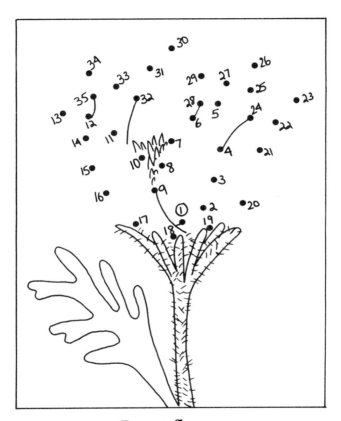

Pasqueflower
Here's a wildflower that's shaped like a cup.

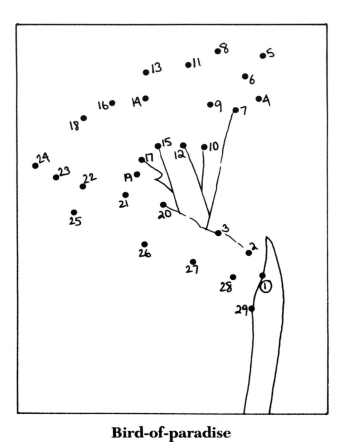

Bird-of-paradise
Think of a beautiful bird when you
look at this flower.

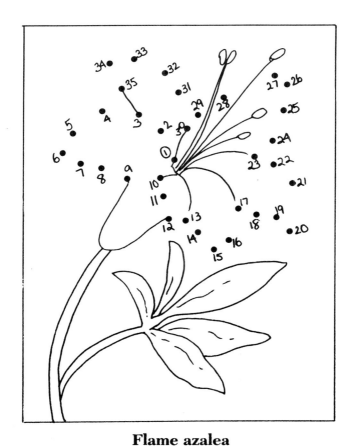

Flame azalea
These flowers are so brightly colored that
they might seem like they're on fire.

25

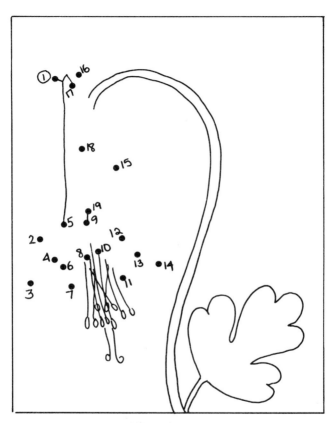

Wild columbine
The petals of this flower sometimes look
like a circle of doves.

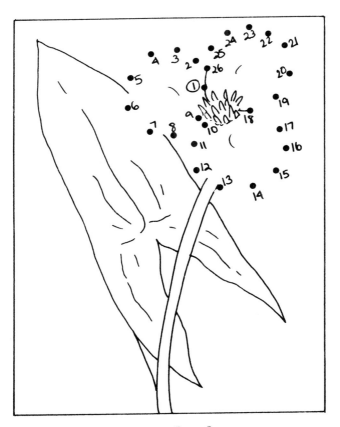

Arrowhead
You can spot these flowers growing in
shallow lakes and slow moving streams.

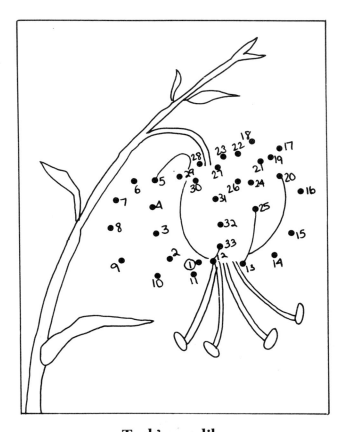

Turk's-cap lily
This tall plant has orange flowers
with red-brown spots.

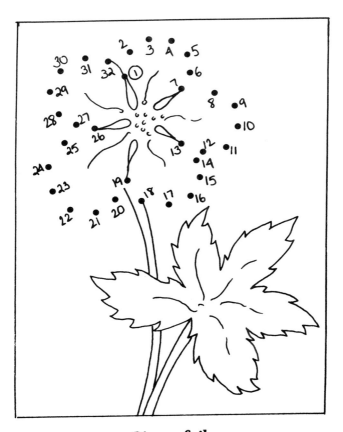

Cinquefoil
The leaves of this flower grow
in 5 round sections.

Dandelion
Some people think this plant is a weed,
but other people love to eat it.

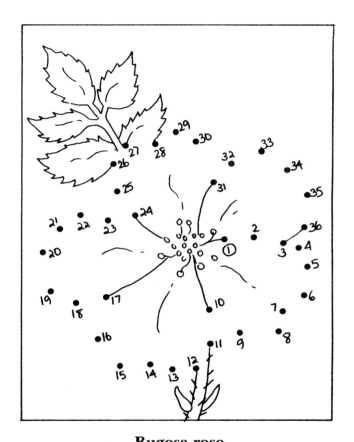

Rugosa rose
This plant, with ruffled pink or white
flowers, grows near the beach.

31

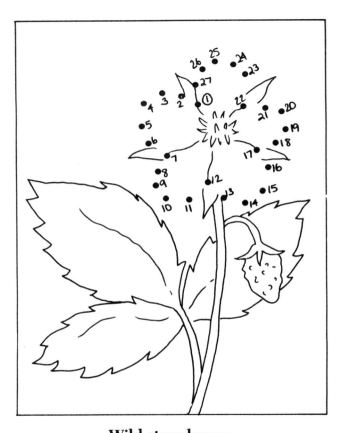

Wild strawberry
This little flower turns into a delicious berry.

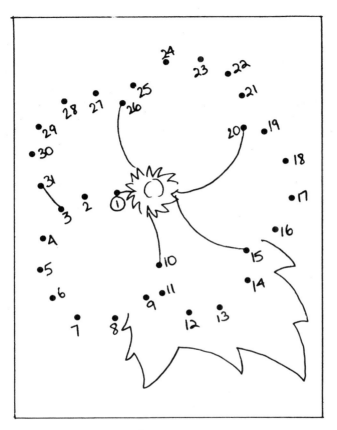

Anemone

Native American people used the root
of this plant to treat wounds.

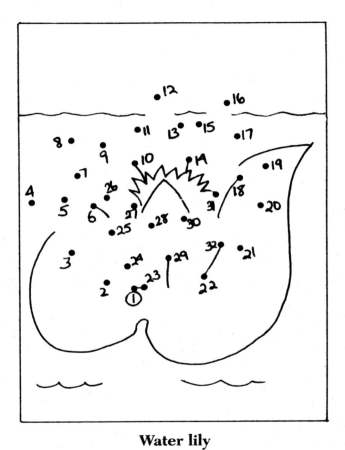

Water lily

Frogs and dragonflies like to sit on the
broad leaves of this water flower.

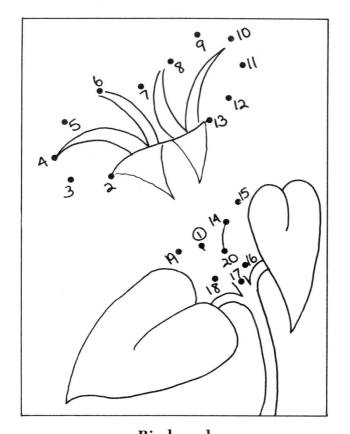

Bindweed
Here's a climbing plant that grows in dry, sandy, and rocky soils.

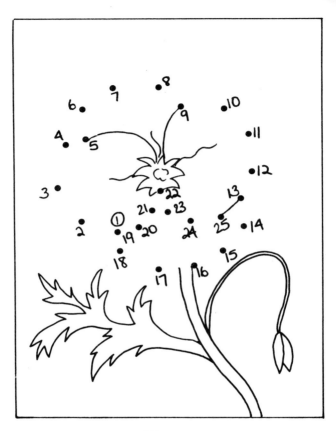

Wild poppy

Dorothy and her friends fell asleep in a field
of these bright red flowers on the way to Oz.

Black-eyed Susan
These bright yellow flowers have
black centers.

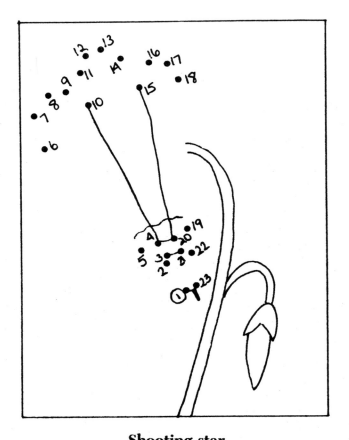

Shooting star
American pioneers used to call these flowers
"prairie pointers."

Carnation
This flower has fringed petals and
tiny, smooth leaves.

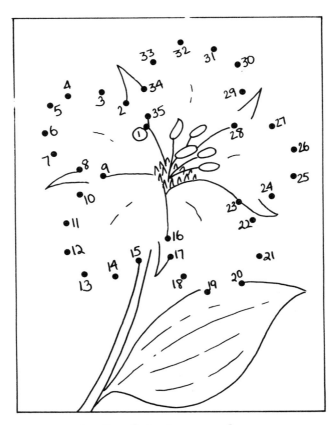

Scarlet pimpernel
This star-like flower blooms in blue,
white, orange, or red.

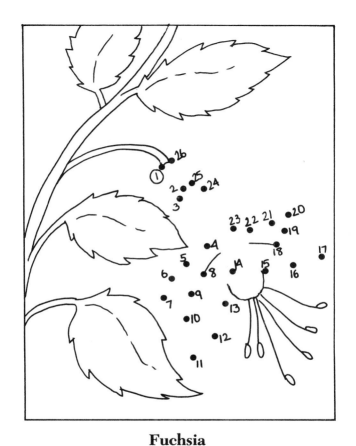

Fuchsia
Here's a delicate flower that grows in
warm parts of the United States.

41

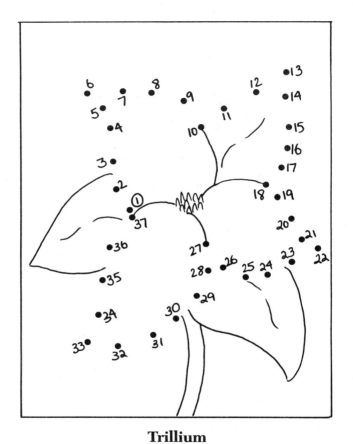

Trillium
This woodland flower is one of spring's early bloomers.

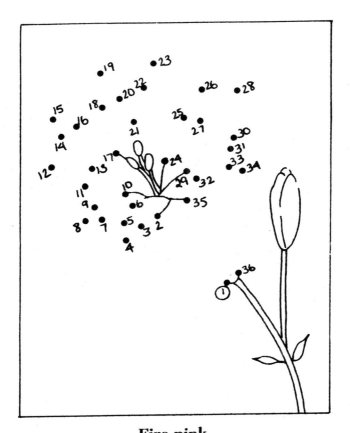

Fire pink
This bright red flower has a sticky stem
that traps insects.

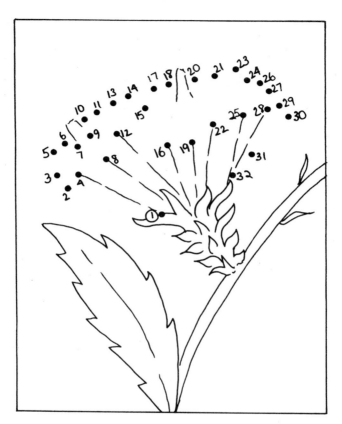

Chicory

The roots of this blue flower are sometimes
used to brew a drink like coffee.

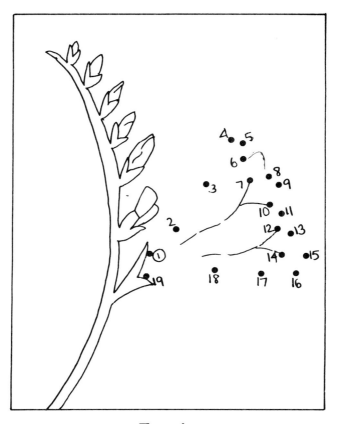

Freesia
This plant, with greenish-yellow flowers,
grows in South Africa.

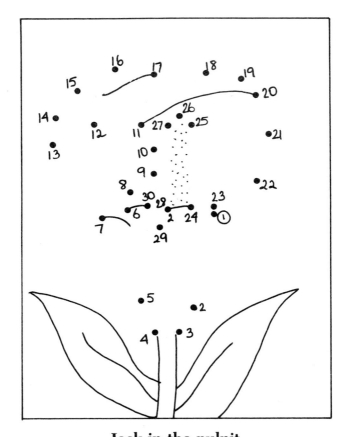

Jack-in-the-pulpit
Here's a spring wildflower that lives in
damp woods and along streams.

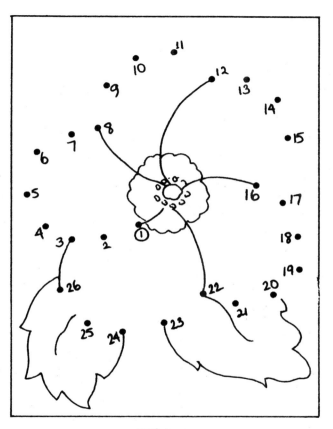

Hibiscus

This plant, which grows where it's very warm, has giant rosy-red flowers.

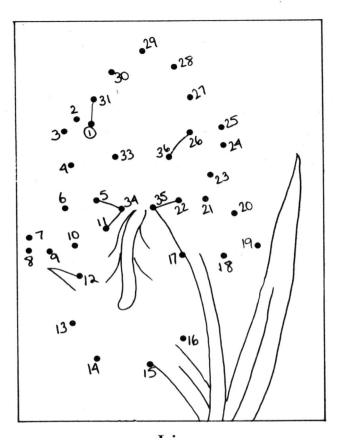

Iris
The flower of this tall plant is often
the color purple.

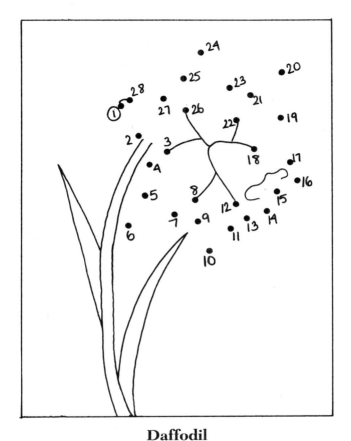

Daffodil
Plant a bulb in the fall to see this cheerful
yellow flower bloom in the spring.

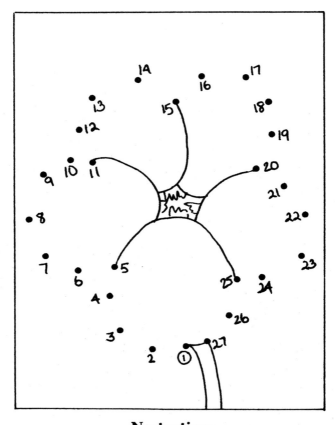

Nasturtium
It's very easy to grow this orange flower
from seed.

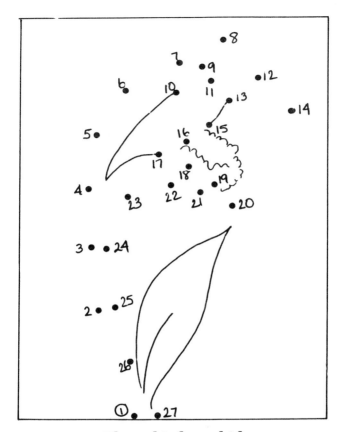

Three-birds orchid
The pink or white flowers of this plant
look like birds in flight.

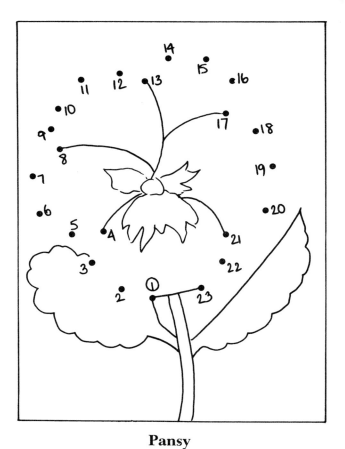

Pansy

With petals soft as velvet, this flower blooms
in many cheerful colors.

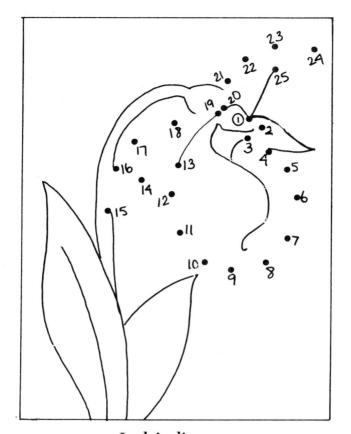

Lady's slipper
The waxy petal on this flower looks
like a slipper.

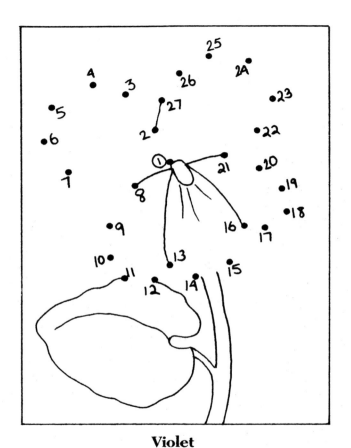

Violet
Here's a dainty, purple flower that grows
in meadows and damp woods.

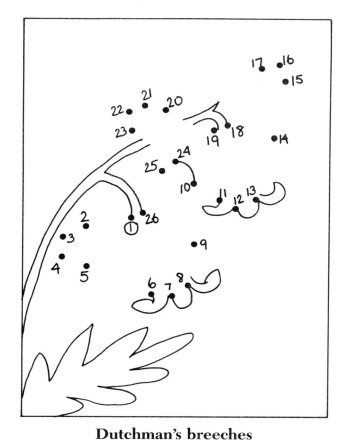

Dutchman's breeches
The little white flowers of this plant look like
pants hanging on a line to dry.

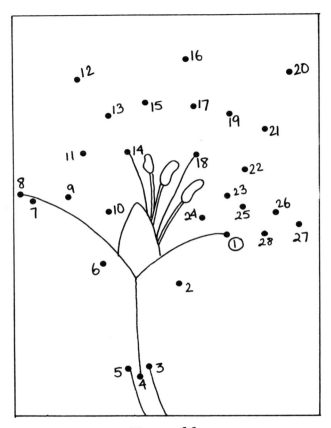

Easter lily
These elegant flowers are white with
touches of pink.

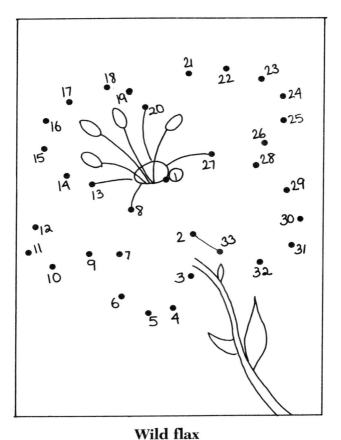

Wild flax
This plant, with blue flowers, often escapes
from gardens to grow in the wild.

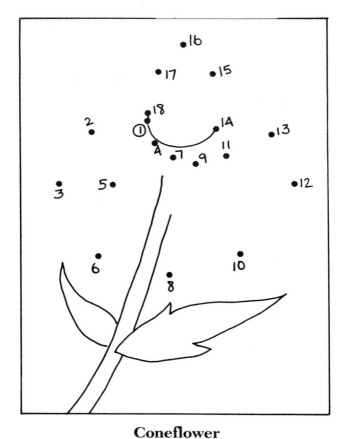

Coneflower
Here's a native American flower that blooms
in purple or yellow.

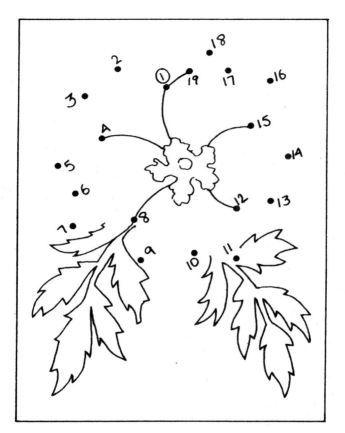

Prairie rose
This roadside and prairie plant has flowers
that bloom in pale pink to white.

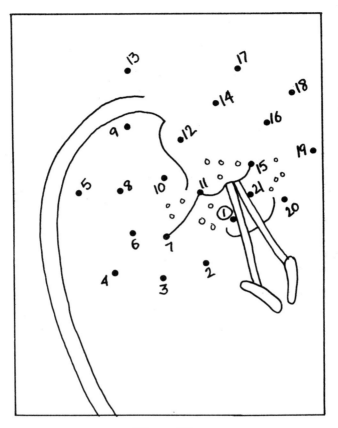

Tiger lily
These orange flowers have red spots.

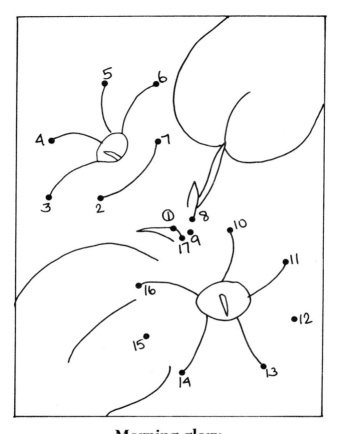

Morning glory
The flowers of this twining plant are
shaped like funnels.

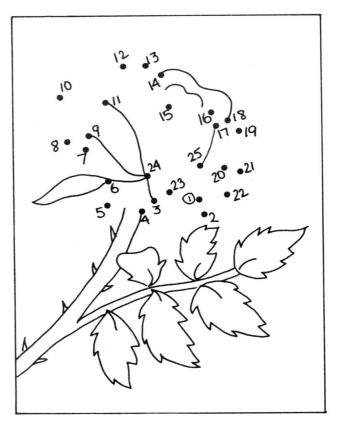

Rose
Many people think that this is the
most beautiful flower in the world.